Help! I'm a Volunteer Youth Worker!

50 EASY TIPS TO HELP YOU SUCCEED WITH KIDS

Doug Fields

Youth Specialties

ZONDERVAN™

GRAND RAPIDS, MICHIGAN 49530

Help! I'm a Volunteer Youth Worker!

50 EASY TIPS TO HELP YOU SUCCEED WITH KIDS

Doug Fields

ZONDERVAN™

GRAND RAPIDS, MICHIGAN 49530

Help! I'm a Volunteer Youth Worker! 50 easy tips to help you succeed with kids

Copyright © 1992 by Youth Specialties, Inc.

Youth Specialties Books, 300 S. Pierce St., El Cajon, CA 92020, are published by
Zondervan, 5300 Patterson Ave., S.E., Grand Rapids, MI 49530

Library of Congress Cataloging-in-Publication Data

Fields, Doug, 1962-
   Help! I'm a volunteer youth worker: 50 easy tips to help you succeed with
kids / Doug Fields.
      p.   cm.
   ISBN: 0-310-57551-6
   1. Church youth workers.   2. Church work with teenagers.   I. Title.
BV447.F54   1992
259'.23—dc20   92-15921
                                                                    CIP

**Published in association with the literary agency of Alive Communications,
Inc., 7680 Goddard Street, Suite 200, Colorado Springs, CO 80920.**

Cover and interior design by Church Art Works

Cartoons by Krieg Barrie

Edited by Joyce Ellis

Printed in the United States of America

07 08 09 10 /❖DC/ 33 32 31 30 29 28 27

Dedication

This book is dedicated to the Page family: John, Karen, Keith, Jody, and Jana. You are all great youth workers in your own special ways. Thanks for all your love, support, and memories. Special thanks to the hundreds of volunteers I've worked with over the years who have invested their time to make young lives count.

Acknowledgments

Though my name appears on the cover of this book, there are several friends who championed the cause to put something short and practical in the hands of volunteers. Tic Long and Noel Becchetti of Youth Specialties first saw the need and believed I could help. Linda Kaye and Noel Veale gave several hours in typing and editing and supported the project. Greg Vujnov, Keith Page, Chris Cannon, and Melinda Douros read the manuscript and shared fresh ideas. And thanks to Steve Williams and Cathy Fields, who are two of the best volunteers I have ever known.

Since the first submittal of this acknowledgment, Steve Williams was tragically killed and taken home on August 18, 1992. He was a valued friend, trusted co-worker, and dedicated volunteer. As a tribute to Steve, Making Young Lives Count has established a Steve Williams Volunteer Memorial that will provide training and resources to other volunteers. If you'd like to make a contribution to this fund or draw from its reserves, please write:

Steve Williams Volunteer Memorial
Making Young Lives Count
4330 Barranca Pkwy, #101–346
Irvine, CA 92714

Introduction

Each time I worked on this book I imagined I was writing to friends with whom I have the privilege of sharing ministry. I want you to feel that I'm a friend sharing with you some of my thoughts, concerns, and ideas about being a volunteer in youth ministry.

Thank you for the role you play as a youth worker! I receive great joy knowing there are thousands of men and women all over our country who are concerned about the spiritual lives of young people and are willing to invest their time in kids. It's comforting to know others are as crazy as I am— willing to volunteer time to express God's love to young people.

As you read through this book, don't become overwhelmed. Fifty ideas are a lot to comprehend, let alone try to implement in your ministry. Try to filter all you read through this one principle: *Something is always better than nothing*. It's true! If you invest only thirty minutes a week in youth ministry, calling kids and letting them know you care about them, you are doing something great. Those thirty minutes won't be forgotten. Please don't feel guilty for what you're not doing, but rejoice and be glad over what you are doing. You are making a difference! Believe it. Again, thank you for all you do. Your reward is waiting!

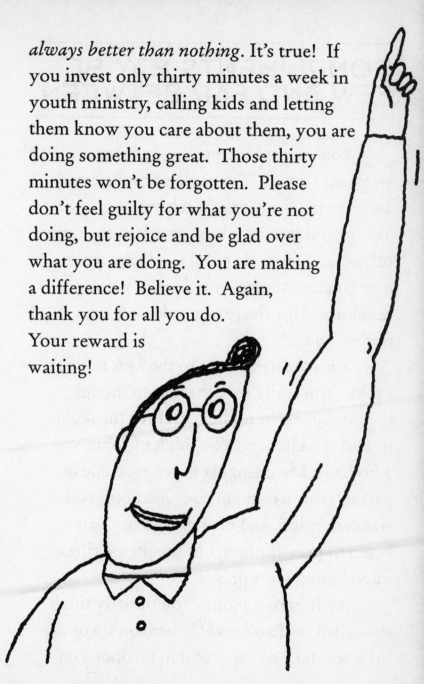

COMPLIMENTS MAY BE FEW AND FAR BETWEEN

You've just returned home from a weekend retreat. You settle onto the couch and give thanks for the weekend's success. You're grateful your boss gave you the time off work. You're thankful God used your new truck to transport kids. Not getting reimbursed for the gasoline doesn't even bother you.

Your thoughts turn to the kids in your cabin. You really love them even though they disappeared in the middle of the night to raid the kitchen. You think of Johnny, who had a life-changing experience due in part to your late-night conversations, constant attention, and unending love. You begin to pray for him, but the phone rings, interrupting your prayer.

It's Johnny's mom. You initially think she called to thank you for her son's wonderful weekend. *Wrong*. Within seconds you

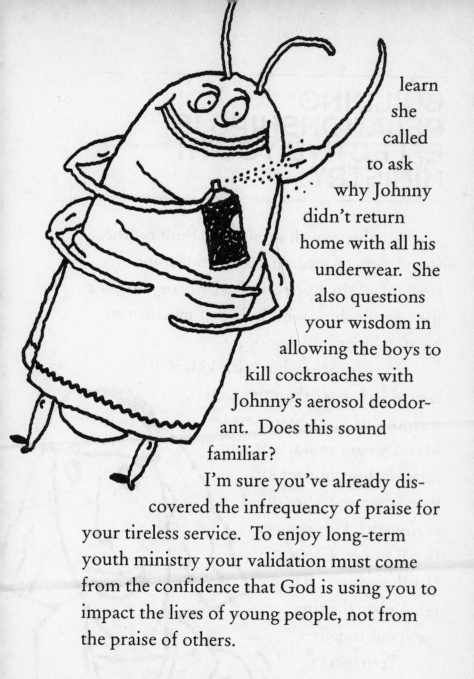

learn she called to ask why Johnny didn't return home with all his underwear. She also questions your wisdom in allowing the boys to kill cockroaches with Johnny's aerosol deodorant. Does this sound familiar?

I'm sure you've already discovered the infrequency of praise for your tireless service. To enjoy long-term youth ministry your validation must come from the confidence that God is using you to impact the lives of young people, not from the praise of others.

BUILDING RELATIONSHIPS IS EFFECTIVE YOUTH MINISTRY

Quality youth ministry is built on the foundation of meaningful relationships. Beyond all the hype and flashy programs, it's the relationships with kids that measure an outstanding youth group.

Your relationship with kids will last years longer than the faint memory of your best message. Messages are important, but relationships impact kids more than speeches do. I *really* wish kids remembered my messages . . . but they don't. They remember the time we spent together.

Teenagers need strong

relationships with adults. Though few admit it, they desire significant relationships with older people. When your kids feel the love you have for them, they will understand your spoken messages about God's love much better.

Build relationships that will continue beyond graduation. It is exciting to watch kids grow and develop, understanding that part of their maturity came from a relationship that a classroom couldn't offer.

CONGRATULATIONS—
YOU'RE A MODEL!

Here's a scary truth: You are constantly communicating a message to the kids you work with. They consciously and unconsciously take note of everything! They watch how you live, how you love the unlovely, how you deal with authority, how you react in difficult situations, how you handle pain, and how you treat your family. They watch because you are a significant adult in their life, and they are looking for answers and direction.

I grew up in a youth ministry with many quality adult leaders. I watched dozens of lessons I've never forgotten. I saw adults love others, give others dignity, and encourage the hurting. These adults didn't need to say, "Doug, let me teach you a lesson on how to care for people." Their lifestyles were a continual curriculum to an impressionable mind and heart. So is yours! Remember, young eyes focus on your life.

FULL-TIME YOUTH MINISTRY ISN'T WHAT IT'S CRACKED UP TO BE

A paid ministry position can seem more glamorous than volunteer work. The impression is that full-time youth work is more fun, constantly affirming, and always filled with quality time with students. Not true! A paid position does not necessarily equal effectiveness. You can often have a more worthwhile ministry as a volunteer than in a paid ministry position.

My wife, Cathy, has a great volunteer ministry. When kids want to talk about problems or important life issues, they approach Cathy. She has deep, meaningful conversations with kids. She can spend her ministry time building significant

relationships while I'm at the office making flyers, returning phone calls, and digging out from under the administrative piles that come with a paid position.

I've met dozens of ex-volunteers who decided seminary and a career change would make their ministry more effective. Most of them were wrong. They ended up disappointed.

As a volunteer, you're the church's most valued treasure. Unless you're confident of God's calling into full-time ministry, remain a volunteer and allow your present employer to finance your youth work.

LET KIDS KNOW THAT YOU BELIEVE IN THEM

Kids have the power to make a difference in this world. They need to know that. Their growing years are filled with self-doubt. They constantly question their existence. You can empower them with four simple words: "I believe in you." These words can transform impressionable adolescents in a world that views them as "excess baggage."

Jesus did this with his disciples. He

looked beyond their sins and inadequacies and said, "I believe in you." That's what he did when he changed Simon's name to Peter, meaning "rock." (I'm assuming Peter's friends thought a more appropriate name would be Sandy or Pebbles!) Then Jesus showed that he believed in Peter. Jesus gave him a vital role in establishing the early church. (Check the book of Acts to see how Peter lived up to Jesus' words.)

Teenagers change when someone believes in them and views them through God's eyes. One day, a female volunteer told Beth that she believed Beth would become a woman of God. At the time, I didn't think much about her comment. But afterwards, Beth told the volunteer that her words became a challenge. That affirmation was a turning point in Beth's life. Beth continues to grow and demonstrate godly qualities. I'm not suggesting that Beth's maturity is solely due to the volunteer's words, but the affirmation gave her strength to pursue a godly lifestyle.

AVAILABILITY IS NEXT TO GODLINESS

We recently asked our youth group if they wanted more Bible studies, more meetings, or more speakers. They said they wanted more opportunities for discussion. Their response reminded me of a simple principle I often forget: Kids have a strong need to talk and be heard.

I have a 72-year-old friend named Marv. He's one of our most loved volunteers because the kids know he is available. He listens. He's not as flashy as the other guys, and he isn't much of a challenge in a foot race. But when kids want to get serious and talk, they look for Marv. He has learned that God had a good reason for giving him two ears and one mouth.

Finding people who are available as good listeners is rare. There's a delicate balance between availability and privacy. Your phone doesn't need to ring all the time, and it's okay to instruct kids to call before they come to your home. Having too many kids wanting to talk to you can be a good problem. It means that you have a gift for listening and you love them enough to be available. Your time is valuable, but when you give your time to someone, you give that person value also.

HELLO, PASTOR

Let's delete the words, "I'm *just* a volunteer" from our vocabulary. If you are caring for kids, you are fulfilling a pastoral responsibility. I realize your denomination or church may not call you a pastor (and that's probably good), but you are not *just* a volunteer. You are a pastor to kids and should begin thinking like one. You may not have the title, but you fulfill the role.

Pastors oversee and attend to the needs of their people. You may not ever teach a Bible study, lead games, or design a promotional flyer, but I encourage you to pastor at least one kid. That one teenager will attend youth group knowing someone loves her. When she's sick, visit her. When she has an important test, pray for her. Care for her as if she were the only kid in your group. You can become the hands and feet of Jesus to her.

LETTERS WILL GET YOU EVERYWHERE

Kids love to get mail! I know teenagers who get excited opening envelopes addressed "Occupant." Most kids are impressed when they get a personal letter—especially from you! Personal letters make kids feel special, knowing you spent the time, energy, and money to send them a letter. They will remember. Often they will save the letter and post it on their bulletin board.

Your letter doesn't have to be a typed, single-spaced novelette. A small piece of stationery with a dozen words is sufficient. For example, "I missed you at youth group. I hope you know I care about you. I can't wait to see you on Sunday." Or, "I drove by your high school the other day and thought of you. I wanted to let you know that I care about you." Or, "It was fun to go to your baseball game. You're great! Give me the schedule for the rest of your season. I would love to go to another game. See ya Sunday."

There is great power behind the few minutes it takes to acknowledge a student in writing. Write a quick letter before today is over. It *will* be worth your time.

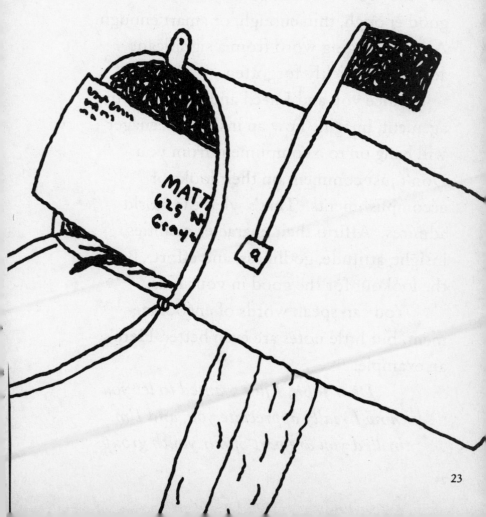

PILE ON THE AFFIRMATION

Kids need affirmation more than they need skits, singing, and special events. Every day they receive messages that they aren't good enough, thin enough, or smart enough. An encouraging word from a significant adult isn't quickly forgotten.

Since you and I need and crave encouragement, imagine how an insecure teenager will hang on to a compliment from you. Don't just comment on their looks or accomplishments. That's what the world admires. Affirm their character qualities, insight, attitude, godliness, and effort. Be on the lookout for the good in your kids.

You can speak words of encouragement, but little notes are even better. Here's an example:

Dear John, I just wanted to let you know I really appreciate you, and I'm thrilled you are part of our youth group.

*I always enjoy seeing you, and I
know God is working in your
life. I can see it!*

If you haven't done
something like this before
or have gotten out of
the habit, try it for a
month. I guarantee
you will see your
ministry change.
If it doesn't,
write to me. I'll
tell you to do
it for another
month.
I know
encourage-
ment works!

CREATIVE CHAUFFEURING CAN CHANGE LIVES

I will never forget Mike's dented, beat-up, ugly, yellow Volkswagen Bug. I would race from the youth room so I'd be the first kid to jump into Mike's car. I always won because no one else wanted to ride in the worst-looking car driven by a youth worker. The other kids in my youth group wanted to ride in the vans and other slick cars.

As an adolescent, I believed there was something special about this car. As an adult, I now know it wasn't the car but the conversation I loved. Mike knew a great principle for youth work: Take advantage of the time in the car.

Driving kids home from programs and picking them up from various events can be a real pain. But think about your car time in a different way. Instead of allowing the kids to search for their favorite radio station, use the drive to get to know them better and talk about the evening's message. It may sound strange, but some of my best youth-group memories took place in a dumpy car with a sensitive youth worker who cared about conversation.

PLAY TOGETHER AS A STAFF

One of the strongest influences on my teenage years was watching my youth leaders play together. They played before various church programs, they attended social events as a group, and they made efforts to be with one another whenever they could.

I was amazed at how much they loved one other and, to be honest, I envied their friendships. I wanted my friends to treat me the way they treated one another. I desperately needed people in my life who cared for

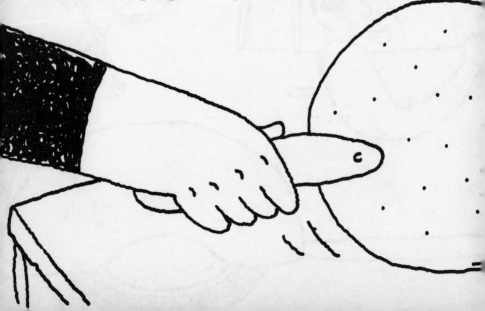

me the way they cared. "If this is how
Christians love one another," I thought,
"then I want to be a Christian." Jesus'
words began to make sense, that others will
know we are his followers by the love we
have for one another (John 13:35).

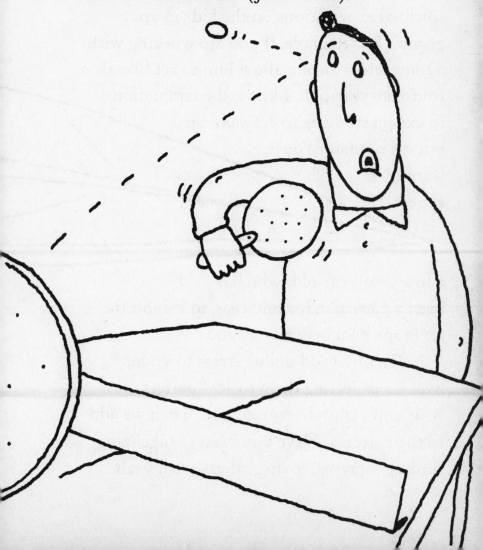

LET YOUR KIDS BE WHO THEY ARE SPIRITUALLY

If you don't want to burn out as a volunteer youth worker, don't place strong spiritual expectations on the kids in your group. For example, if you are working with a fourteen-year-old, allow him to act like a fourteen-year-old. I know the temptation to expect students to act *your* age, but it's not fair. You shouldn't expect

a fourteen-year-old, who has been a Christian for one year, to exhibit the same spiritual maturity as you.

We often add undue stress to young lives by expecting them to act "perfect." Kids enter church stressed out. Then we add to their stress: "Have you been evangelizing, reading, praying, loving others? Oh yeah,

I'm glad you're here." Kids sense our expectations, and they can stress out trying to please us.

Remember, you are working with *young* people. When we were teenagers, we couldn't sit still. We loved throwing paper airplanes. That's the job description of an adolescent. Encouraging maturity in kids' relationships with Christ is important,

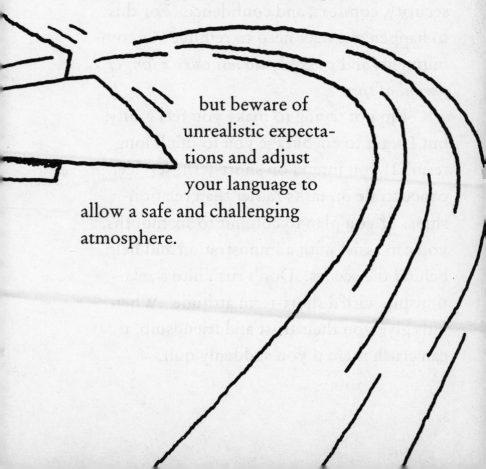

but beware of unrealistic expectations and adjust your language to allow a safe and challenging atmosphere.

LONG-TERM YOUTH MINISTRY HAS GREAT REWARDS

Kids have adults coming in and out of their lives all the time. I'd love to see youth ministry become a place for adult consistency—a place where kids feel a sense of security, comfort, and confidence. For this to happen, we may need to rethink our commitments and possibly *do less over a longer period of time.*

I'm not trying to make you feel guilty, but I want to encourage you to think long term. If you intend on short-term service, concentrate on tasks rather than relationships. If you plan to commit to six months, you can assist with administration and help behind the scenes. Don't rush into a relationship with a short-term attitude. When kids give you their trust and friendship, it can crush them if you suddenly quit.

I'm not suggesting that you pledge the rest of your life to youth ministry, but the longer your commitment, the more influential your ministry will be.

RECRUIT FELLOW SUCKERS . . . ER, VOLUNTEERS

Finding quality helpers for youth ministry is one of the toughest tasks I know. Your connections within your church may be fresh contacts for your director.

Some of the best recruiters I've known have been other volunteers. Some of your friends who aren't involved within the youth

ministry may wonder, "How can you have so much fun with teenagers?" Let them in on the secret. Invite them to observe the action. You'll also find yourself having more fun as you share this experience with your friends.

Find out how you can best help with the ongoing recruiting process. You may not have great success, but the fact that you're assisting in a tough process will be a great blessing to your director.

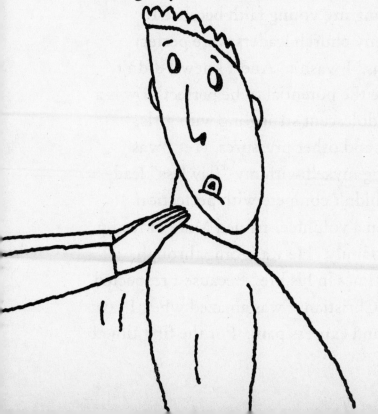

LET KIDS SEE WHO YOU ARE

As you build relationships with kids, it's crucial that they recognize you are human. Simply because you are a youth leader, some kids believe you are destined to sit next to Jesus. This may sound strange, but some kids think you're perfect.

When I was a sophomore, I considered abandoning my young faith because I thought my church leaders were perfect Christians. I wasn't. And I knew I didn't even have the potential to be perfect. I was a normal adolescent struggling with girls, cheating, and other pressures. Yet I was comparing myself with my "flawless" leaders. I couldn't compete with perfection.

Then a volunteer named Mike moved in with my family. He was going through difficult times in his life. Because I respected him as a Christian, I was amazed when I saw him cry and express pain. For the first time I observed a Christian adult with problems. "Mike has problems like me," I thought, "yet he's a Christian leader. I can be like Mike." His transparency literally changed my life.

You don't have to hang out all your dirty laundry or share your grossest sins with kids. But allow them to know that you also have struggles, and encourage them to pray for you. They need to know they are not alone—adults screw up, too. This gives them hope!

SHOW OFF YOUR MARRIAGE

Our world desperately needs quality Christian marriages. Most kids grow up in broken families and have pathetic snapshots of married life. They live with parents who have pessimistic attitudes about matrimony. It's a fact that many marriages aren't making it, and kids are looking for hopeful examples.

If you are married, remember that kids are watching how you treat your spouse. Yours may be the only good marriage they ever observe. It's vital for them to see spouses loving one another. I want teenage guys in my group thinking, "I want to marry a woman who loves her husband like Cathy does." I want girls saying, "I want to marry somebody who treats me the way Doug treats Cathy."

If you have a good marriage, show it off. If your marriage is hurting, maybe it's time to take a break from youth ministry and renew your relationship so you won't become part of the negative statistics.

LOOK AFTER NEW VOLUNTEERS

Do you remember how you felt your first few weeks as a volunteer? How long did you feel out of place? What was it that finally made you feel comfortable? Who encouraged you? Ignored you? Introduced you to kids? Do you still feel out of place?

You can perform a valuable ministry to an unsure volunteer. You can bring great comfort to new staff people by taking them under your wing and introducing them to kids who will help them feel comfortable.

Greg had been a volunteer in our group for two years when he began caring for new volunteers. One Sunday morning he met Linda, a new woman volunteer. Since I was busy with programming details, he took the responsibility to welcome her. He introduced her to other staff and kids and sat with her during the program. To make a long story short, Linda felt so welcomed that she soon fell in love with Greg and married him a year later. (Caring for new volunteers may have several benefits!)

EXPRESS YOURSELF

God wants to use you in your areas of giftedness. If you've been blessed with a skill, craft, or passion, you can use it to enhance your ministry.

Misha had a passion for rest homes and caring for the aged. I personally don't feel comfortable in rest homes. I don't like the smells there or the sight of dying people. I get depressed thinking about my aging parents. But Misha's love for the elderly complements my weakness. Her enthusiasm encourages kids to get involved in a ministry to the elderly.

Take the initiative to express your gift-edness and interests. Your youth director is probably swamped and may not encourage new ideas, especially if it's going to add to an already full schedule. Be prepared to explain the benefits of your idea. Take the responsibility to make it happen. It's much easier for supervisors to okay good ideas that won't add to their work load. I like my volunteers to submit dreams which grow out of their giftedness. Don't be afraid to do the same.

SMALL IS BEAUTIFUL

Beware of this myth: The bigger the programs the better your youth group. Numbers give the impression of success. The truth is, bigger isn't always better.

We recently sponsored an outreach event that drew hundreds of neighboring kids. When we had more kids than we expected, we began to panic. We ordered more food, drinks, and supplies. The turnout was huge, but the program wasn't all that great. Actually, it was *too* big. The best part of

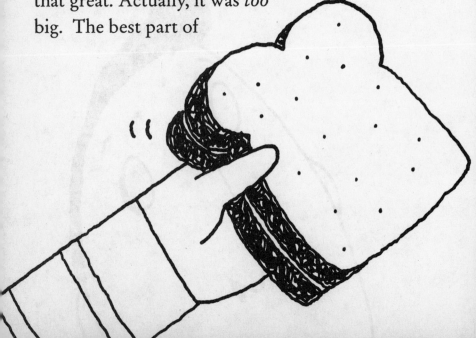

the program was when ten kids took the excess food to the inner city and distributed it to the homeless. The men and women living on the streets were incredibly thankful, and the kids experienced something they will never forget.

I will never forget that night either. It reminds me that bigger isn't always better. Our new homeless friends would say the same.

BECOME A STUDENT

I'd rather have one teachable volunteer than ten volunteers with no interest in growing and maturing. It's fairly easy to find volunteers who will stop kids from throwing pizza at the windows or burning the church down. But it's tough to recruit volunteers who desire to learn.

You can model a teachable spirit by reading, listening to tapes, and attending training seminars. I love the following quote: "Be green and grow, or you'll become ripe and rot." A green volunteer is a great volunteer.

IT'S OKAY IF YOU AREN'T LIKED BY EVERYONE

To this day, I still don't like to admit that there are kids, parents, and other leaders who don't like me.

The fact is that if you're a leader and you're making or enforcing decisions that affect others, you won't always be liked. Some of your decisions are going to rub people the wrong way. This is true with any leadership position. Instead of trying to run from responsibility, work toward fairness. You'll feel a lot better when you realize that everyone isn't going to agree with you. And you'll be in great company. The Scriptures are clear—Jesus wasn't liked by everyone either.

STEER CLEAR OF THE COMPARISON TRAP

The comparison trap is easy to fall into. For example, you may believe another volunteer is up front too often, and you'd enjoy a more visible leadership position. Or you may be jealous of another volunteer who seems to attract the "fun" kids. Comparisons are common, but no one wins.

Kids need volunteers with diverse gifts and talents, volunteers with differing skills, interests, and personalities. I don't know anything about computers, modems, network systems, or megabytes, but some of the kids in my group live in that computer world. I have a difficult time reaching them. Fortunately, we have a 50-year-old volunteer who speaks computer jargon, and those kids love him.

Don't waste energy wishing kids would relate to you if you were a better speaker, funnier, or more athletic. Allow your personalized abilities to passionately reach and care for kids. Permit God to use what he has given you.

BE CAREFUL WITH AFFECTION

A good rule of thumb is: Female volunteers spend the majority of their time caring for girls, and male volunteers spend their time with guys. This simple guideline helps control potentially dangerous sexual situations. The sexual attraction between adults and students is an issue we must continually address and deal with in our ministries.

Several years ago, someone suggested that I evaluate my relationships with kids and take note of those who received my affection. He believed I was consistent in hugging* girls who were cute, fun, and popular while the quieter girls either got waves or handshakes. At first I became defensive, but after more thought, I agreed with his observation. I never consciously set out to hug only the "pretty-types," but they seemed more aggressive and physical with their feelings. By not being consistent with my affection, though, I reinforced the world's message that "pretty" people get all the attention. In this mixed-up world we need to constantly be alert, thoughtful, and consistent with our affection.

*There are differing opinions within the Christian community over hugging. I believe kids need nonsexual affection from caring adults. Without being too legalistic, I suggest my volunteers hug the opposite sex from the side.

YOU DON'T HAVE TO BE A PARENT

Your function as a youth worker is to build relationships, encourage spiritual maturity, and model a Christian lifestyle. Your role isn't that of parent. Kids are interested in a relationship with a significant adult who loves them and takes them seriously. They aren't looking for more parents.

I know many parents who are intimidated by youth workers because they feel youth workers are trying to replace them as parents. The truth is, you will never be a parent to these kids. If you try to play a parental role, you can become a divisive wedge between parents and their children.

Cherish your role as friend, and be thankful you're *not* their parent.

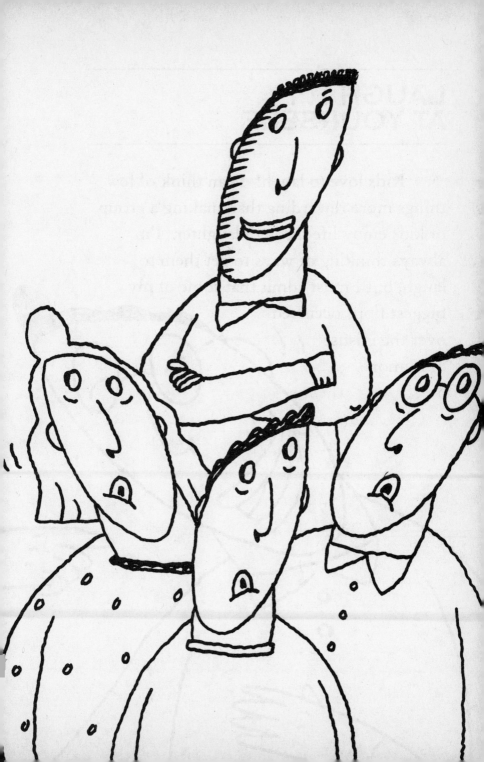

LAUGH . . .
AT YOURSELF

Kids love to laugh! I can think of few
things more rewarding than making a group
of kids enjoy life through laughter. I'm
always thinking of ways to get them to
laugh, but I must admit that some of my
biggest flops occurred
over the misuse
of humor.

It's easy to make kids laugh when you make fun of their friends or you isolate one or two and embarrass them. I'll never forget making a comment about a girl's new dress. I joked about how the dress reminded me of the Partridge Family bus. Everyone laughed. It was a funny comment because the dress *did* look like their bus. I didn't think much about the remark until I later saw her crying as she talked with my wife. My attempt at humor embarrassed her and wounded her dignity. I felt awful.

I've discovered that using humor at *my* expense is better than making fun of kids. If I put anyone down for the sake of humor, I make sure it's me. This is tough for me since I'm fairly quick witted and my mouth often works faster than my discernment. We can work at this one together.

YOUR OCCASIONAL FRUSTRATIONS MAY HAVE TO DO WITH THE LACK OF TRAINING, ORGANIZATION, AND DIRECTION OF THE DIRECTOR

I'm sure you've experienced your share of discouraging times. I can relate to your frustrations. But part of your disappointment may come from your director's lack of organization, direction, planning, and training. This is normal.

Most youth workers aren't prepared to deal with the realities of professional ministry. We learn on the job and pray that we'll have more accomplishments than mistakes. My volunteers get frustrated when I don't know what I'm doing. If you can relate to those feelings, you're not alone.

In seminary, I had classes in Greek, Hebrew, New Testament, and theology. But

I was never privileged with classes on how to deal with people, how to administrate, how to minister to hyperactive teenagers, or how to get parents off your . . .

Expect your director to be growing and learning, but don't demand that he or she have it all together. The learning curve in youth ministry goes straight up. We all have a lot to learn! By keeping your expectations reasonable, you will feel better about your ministry and experience less frustration. Be patient and encouraging. Join the team of learners.

BE SENSITIVE TO VOLUNTEER PARENTS

Please don't expect the same type of enthusiasm and commitment from volunteers with children as from volunteers with no children. Volunteers with children don't love the ministry any less.

They simply have less time and freedom. (I can hear the volunteers with children shouting, "Amen! Finally someone understands.")

Instead of wishing these volunteer parents were around more often, encourage them. Overwhelm them with thanks any time they serve. Offer to baby-sit for them. Help them attend a youth event they would normally miss because of their children.

We need more parents modeling family life for our kids. Allow them the privilege of putting their families before youth ministry.

NAME-DROPPING ALLOWED HERE

For most kids, their name is their greatest possession. Remembering a teenager's name communicates significance. The kids probably won't remember your name, but if you remember theirs, you'll show them you're glad they came and you think they're someone of worth.

During my adolescent years I frequently attended a youth group where many of the adults called the kids "brother" or "sister." At first I thought this was a clever way to communicate the theology of family, but I later realized that the adults didn't remember our names.

I'll never forget the one man who took time to remember my name. I wasn't even in his small group. I don't remember having a significant conversation with him, but he cared enough to remember my greatest possession. You can do the same thing.

TAKE INITIATIVE

A volunteer who takes initiative is greatly appreciated. Being motivated even in little things is a great help—from cleaning up after an event to making phone calls to visitors.

It can be difficult working with volunteers who don't act on anything until they receive "orders." Make yourself more helpful. Before you're asked, go ahead and do something you *know* needs to be done.

I'm always delighted when I ask a volunteer to help me with a certain project and she tells me, "I already did it." After I recover from the shock, I give thanks for the volunteers who take initiative.

SOUL CHECK

Did you know that your inner life communicates as much as your actions? Take a minute to think about your inner health. How is your love for God? How is your thought life? How is your integrity? How is your devotional life?

Take time to reflect on the messages your inner life sends. If you don't feel comfortable with those messages, take appropriate action. Make changes. Kids are looking for something to emulate. Your life message can be just that.

WANTED: MEMORY MAKERS

Providing memories for kids is vital. So many of them feel lost. They don't have a positive view of themselves. They have little attachment with their past. Teens are constantly questioning their identity and their existence.

Some of the best gifts we can give them during these turbulent years are positive memories. Such memories provide comfort and build a foundation for their future. It's great to be able to look back on positive memories.

We can't protect kids from all negative

experiences or bad memories. But when they experience pain, we must trust God to do the impossible in their lives while we work on the possible. Part of doing the possible is planning experiences that will ensure strong memories. You are a memory maker!

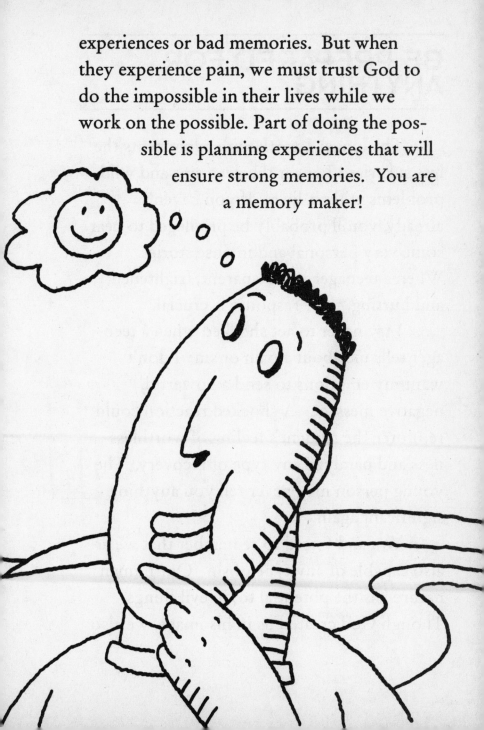

BE PREPARED FOR ANYTHING

The longer I work with adolescents the less surprised I am at the deep sins and wild problems in their lives. If you haven't already, you'll probably be privileged to hear some very personal and intense stories. When a teenager is transparent, frightened, and hurting, your response is crucial.

I try never to act shocked when a teenager tells me about a pain or sin. I don't want my emotions to send a powerful, negative message. A shocked reaction could reinforce the student's feeling of worthlessness and paralyze any type of recovery. The young person may never tell you anything significant again.

You and I need to remember that we are also capable of any type of sin. Our human nature has the potential to do evil things. Though God created us in his image, we also possess a wicked nature, capable of doing anything.

You may find some of your best kids involved in any situation from pregnancy to the occult. Hurt with them. Cry with them. Be heartbroken with them. But don't be shocked by their sins. Spend more time being shocked by God's grace and continual forgiveness. And help your kids find it.

KEEP AN EYE ON THE BIG PICTURE

One mark of a quality youth ministry is your ability to articulate why you do what you do. If you can't explain the philosophy and vision of your youth ministry, you need to get together with someone who can. Your understanding will not only help your youth director be more effective, but it will also help you focus your personal time and energy. If no one has a vision, get together with others and create one.

When you understand your philosophy and vision, work to maintain it. If you don't

agree with it, express your feelings and seek a better understanding of it. If you still differ with your leaders, find another place within the church, or find another church whose philosophy and vision you can support. You probably won't be able to change the vision God has given the leaders. You will spend more time fighting than ministering.

LITTLE THINGS CAN MEAN A LOT

Christianity desperately needs men and women who will be faithful in small things. Small things are actions requiring work without returning praise. Our world encourages the bigger-is-better mentality and discourages servanthood.

God rewards those who are faithful in the small things. Our youth ministries would be more effective if they were completely staffed with men and women who were satisfied with doing small things.

Jeff, a faithful volunteer, does the tasks no one else wants to do. He paints the youth room, he helps clean while other volunteers are leading games, and he talks with the kids who usually resist conversation. At first I didn't understand why kids loved Jeff so much. He didn't

have up-front responsibilities, and I didn't think many knew him.

But I recently read this verse: "Whoever can be trusted with very little can also be trusted with much" (Luke 16:10). I immediately thought of Jeff and understood why his ministry is effective.

CONSISTENCY IS BEAUTIFUL

One of the characteristics I appreciate most in a volunteer is *consistency*. If you are consistent, you support your director in a tremendous way. I would rather have one person I could always count on than a dozen inconsistent volunteers. Consistency communicates your commitment to a mission as well as to a team of people.

The word *consistency*, however, doesn't mean

overcommitment. Don't volunteer for every program your youth ministry offers. It's difficult to be consistent when you're expected to be at every event. Make a commitment to the programs appropriate for your time and talents. Then be consistent in that commitment. Don't waste time feeling guilty for what you're not doing. Be grateful to God for what you can do. And be glad that you've made a commitment to be counted on.

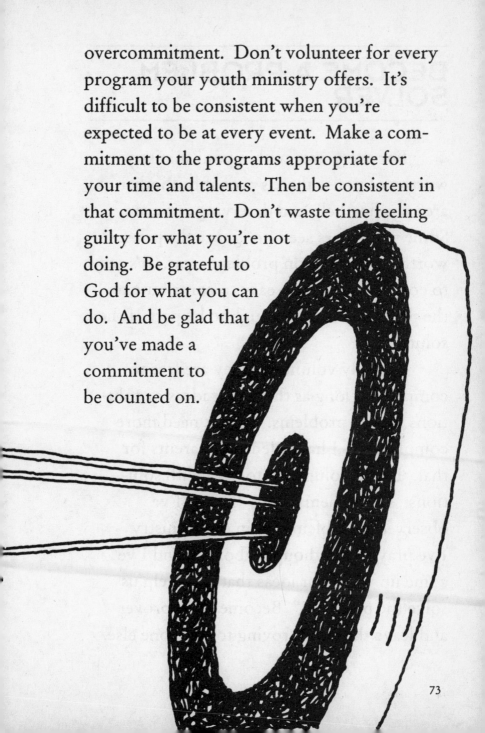

BECOME A PROBLEM SOLVER

For every area within your ministry worthy of praise there's probably another area needing help and deserving criticism. Some volunteers seem to ignore the praise-worthy and focus on problem areas. It's easy to complain. It's also easy to contribute to the problem. But it's tough to be part of the solution.

I tell my volunteers they are free to complain as long as they offer ideas or solutions for the problems. I don't need more complainers. I have plenty of parents for that. I need volunteers to help with solutions. I love them to say, "Doug, I've observed a problem within our ministry. I've prayed and thought about it, and I've come up with four ideas that may help us solve the problem." Become an improver and leave the disapproving to someone else.

SUPPORT YOUR LOCAL DIRECTOR

Your youth director needs your affirmation—both verbally and nonverbally. Support this person's actions and decisions. Show her your loyalty. Talk positively about her in front of kids, parents, and other church leaders.

It has meant so much when I've heard that a volunteer supported me when someone else was attacking me. (It's common for church people to be critical and negative.)

When was the last time you told your director she is doing a great job? It will make a big difference in your relationship. I can live with confidence for a week on one supportive compliment. Don't let this week run out without sharing good words with your supervisor.

GET BELOW THE SURFACE

Most youth workers find it easier to talk to kids about sports, school, the weather, and friends than about spiritual issues. Many fall into a pattern of relying on the senior pastor or director to provide the spiritual input. It's simple to scratch the surface with conversation, but it's tough to dig deeper and challenge them in their faith.

Kids want to be challenged in their faith. They live with many questions and fears and are looking for direction and insight. They need your help, spiritual instruction, and accountability to practice their Christian faith. (With those expectations, though, see page 30, "Let Your Kids Be Who They Are Spiritually.)

Most adolescents graduate high school without having a personal relationship with God. Their teen years are a time of tossing back and forth with uncertainty partially because significant adults aren't caring for them and giving them spiritual direction. Don't wait for someone else to challenge your kids spiritually. If you don't do it, it may never happen.

BECOME A TREASURE HUNTER

I'm constantly amazed at the resources available to my volunteers. Their contacts in the marketplace are so different from mine.

I was an expert at complaining about the things we didn't have for our youth ministry. But once I stopped complaining and started asking, I found my volunteers had incredible contacts and could get almost anything we needed. One volunteer knew a floor contractor who was willing to donate carpet and installation. Another volunteer knew a woodworker who built us a stage. Another had a friend at a soft-drink dispenser company who now gives us free soft drinks for outreach events. All we did was put the word out.

I'm convinced that people want to contribute to something significant. Many people love the opportunity to use their skills and materials to make a difference in the world. And they are often more than willing to donate them to a good cause.

VISIT KIDS ON THEIR TURF

Kids love to see you on their campus. At first, they may be shocked and ask twenty questions about why you're there. But they will be thrilled you took the time to visit their turf.

Each school district has its own policies about adults on campus. But even on a closed campus, you can visit a sporting event or arts performance after school hours. If you work a nine-to-five shift, you may find a lunch visit your only option. Take advantage of their lunch break and eat on their territory, or meet them at the local fast-food restaurant they frequent.

Although your time on campus may be brief, it's a great way to communicate your interest in their world.

FOCUS ON FOLLOW-UP

One of the toughest tasks of a youth ministry team is tracking and caring for its young people. Without proper follow-up, kids can easily get lost and fall into the hole of forgotten names and faces. The larger your group, the more difficult the task.

Effective follow-up involves an active concern for what's happening in kids' lives. Their world is so overwhelming that they need someone to make it small—noticing when something is wrong, caring about their mood swings, being concerned about their successes and failures, and noticing when they miss youth group.

Quality follow-up communicates the ABC's—*acceptance*, *belonging*, and being *cared for*. It's amazing to watch a young person who doesn't feel good about himself come into contact with a person or a group of people who begin to show him love by giving consistent injections of the ABC's.

I've watched young people with low self-esteem grow in their faith and confidence because someone took the time to follow them up. Kids need you to be crazy about their personal world.

MAINTAIN SOME "ESCAPE FRIENDS"

The only friendships many youth ministry volunteers have are those within their church and youth ministry. These friendships are essential to building a good team, but maintaining outside friendships may be the key to your staying power. It's much easier to burn out and

lose enthusiasm when your world consists of only youth ministry people.

I need good friends outside of our youth ministry who don't care whether I didn't teach the curriculum well and aren't concerned about the obnoxious kids I found swimming in the baptismal. These friends can't relate to my youth-ministry problems, but they care about me, my life, and my marriage. I need these friends. They keep me fresh. They remind me there's more to life than our youth ministry.

YOU CAN BE THE SPARK PLUG FOR YOUR MINISTRY

During low times in our youth program, it's usually an enthusiastic volunteer who reignites our spark. Last summer a college student named Rand joined our tired volunteer team. I couldn't seem to get the troops excited about anything. But because Rand was a peer volunteer, his enthusiasm differed from mine, and he was able to fan their flame. He had new ideas. His eager body language and electrified voice changed our attitudes and our meetings.

While we were discussing details of ministry, as soon as Rand started talking I found myself sitting up, more alert. He'd say, "It's so great to be with kids isn't it? It's so fun to . . ." At first I wanted to tell him to relax and mellow out. I'm glad I didn't. Rand's enthusiasm changed the dynamics of our staff.

Every youth ministry team needs a
spark plug who will excite the workers
when they get
weary.

ASK FOR EVALUATION

Periodic review of your effectiveness will help both you and your director. Don't be afraid to ask for an evaluation. It is worth the time it takes, considering the amount of time you volunteer. Tell your director that you want to know what you do well and what you don't do as well.

When I perform reviews, I evaluate volunteers' effectiveness by these criteria: their *attitude*, their *performance*, and their *fit* within the ministry.

Attitude is the most important because it is more difficult to change than performance and fit. Performance and fit can be adapted, worked on, and modified. A positive attitude can't be taught, yet it is more valuable than any amount of "performing" you can do.

REMEMBER THE "OTHER" KIDS

Too often, we're concerned only with the spirituality of *our* kids. Pressure from senior pastors and parents to "take care of our own" often results in a holy-huddle mentality. But when this style of ministry becomes our sole focus, we lose sight of the majority of our audience—kids outside the church.

It's safe to assume that less than 25 percent of all young people attend youth groups. This means a lot of kids aren't in church. There will never be any competition with other youth groups until every teenager is involved in at least one.

As a volunteer, you can help model this thinking. If you're involved with an inward-looking youth group, challenge the leadership to look outward as you continue caring for the kids God has entrusted to you.

BARBECUE SOME SACRED COWS

A sacred cow might be a program or tradition that is continued because it has always been done that way. An example of a sacred cow might be the meeting room you've always met in and the chairs that have always been in rows because the founding senior pastor (who has been dead for twenty years) loved people to sit in rows. If your group has sacred cows, help barbecue them. Sacred cows can hinder the effectiveness of your youth ministry.

Kids and their needs are changing all the time. If we are still doing the same things we did ten years ago, we may be planning and programming for kids who don't exist.

Measure your traditions against your audience. Begin taking action. Make hamburger from your sacred cows.

DEPEND ON GOD

This may appear obvious, and I don't want to make light of a serious theological concept. But many people heavily involved in God's work forget to consult him about their projects.

Dependence on God will make a difference in your personal life, the youth ministry, and the kids you work with. It's no secret that things work better when God is a part of them.

Youth workers need to ask God to use them in the ways *he* wants. This may include stuffing bulletins, greeting kids as they come in, or caring for only one kid. If God is directing your life and ministry, you'll be rewarded in whatever you do.

SEEK TO RESOLVE CONFLICT

Most kids don't know how to resolve conflict. I never took a class in conflict resolution, did you? Whether we know it or not, we're modeling conflict management every time a conflict arises. When kids approach you to complain or gossip, you have a superb opportunity to help them deal with their tensions and lead them toward resolution.

No one loves conflicts. Take steps to resolve them as soon as you feel tension. Since you can't avoid all tensions, you will begin to build ammunition if there isn't speedy reconciliation.

Godly people are not free from conflict. Jesus started it, ended it, and avoided it—but he was around it. Another example of biblical conflict is the argument between Paul and Barnabas over John's presence on a missionary journey (Acts 15:36–41). They resolved their conflict and went their separate ways. You may have to do the same thing, but make peaceful settlement your goal.

COMPLEMENT YOUR DIRECTOR'S WEAK SPOTS

Your director has weaknesses. We all do. One of the key elements of working as a team is admitting our personal weaknesses and allowing others to surround them with their strengths. Imagine the potential of a youth staff who allow each other to counter weaknesses with strengths.

I recently talked with a youth pastor who has bitter feelings toward one of his volunteers. This particular volunteer spends much of her ministry time building relationships with students. He doesn't like to spend a lot of time with kids because his gifts are more administrative than relational. This youth pastor is tense and bitter because his kids like the volunteer more than him. But we all need to remember that differing gifts can be complementary rather than competitive.

WELCOME KIDS HOME

The father in the story of the Prodigal Son (Luke 15:11–32) is one of my heroes. I admire him. He welcomed his sinful son home, embraced him, and threw a party. His attitude of appreciation in the midst of pain has impacted my ministry to young people.

The son returned home with guilt and remorse over his extravagant and sinful lifestyle. Had his father greeted him with condemnation and anger, healing would have been delayed or even destroyed. Instead, I'm sure the son immediately remembered his family's warmth and unconditional acceptance.

This story illustrates how we should treat kids who temporarily leave their faith and/or the youth group. Our response to lost and guilty kids can determine how they view the church, Christianity, and God. Welcome prodigal kids with sincere warmth. Instead of saying, "Where have you been?" or "I haven't seen you in a long time," say, "It's great to see you! I've missed you." *Every* kid needs to feel welcome.

RESOURCES FROM YOUTH SPECIALTIES

Professional Resources
Administration, Publicity, & Fundraising (Ideas Library)
Developing Student Leaders
Equipped to Serve: Volunteer Youth Worker Training Course
Help! I'm a Junior High Youth Worker!
Help! I'm a Small-Group Leader!
Help! I'm a Sunday School Teacher!
Help! I'm a Volunteer Youth Worker!
How to Expand Your Youth Ministry
How to Speak to Youth...and Keep Them Awake at the Same Time
Junior High Ministry (Updated & Expanded)
The Ministry of Nurture: A Youth Worker's Guide to Discipling Teenagers
One Kid at a Time: Reaching Youth through Mentoring
Purpose-Driven Youth Ministry
So That's Why I Keep Doing This! 52 Devotional Stories for Youth Workers
A Youth Ministry Crash Course
The Youth Worker's Handbook to Family Ministry

Youth Ministry Programming
Camps, Retreats, Missions, & Service Ideas (Ideas Library)
Compassionate Kids: Practical Ways to Involve Your Students in Mission
    and Service
Creative Bible Lessons from the Old Testament
Creative Bible Lessons in 1 & 2 Corinthians
Creative Bible Lessons in John: Encounters with Jesus
Creative Bible Lessons in Romans: Faith on Fire!
Creative Bible Lessons on the Life of Christ
Creative Junior High Programs from A to Z, Vol. 1 (A-M)
Creative Junior High Programs from A to Z, Vol. 2 (N-Z)
Creative Meetings, Bible Lessons, & Worship Ideas (Ideas Library)
Crowd Breakers & Mixers (Ideas Library)
Drama, Skits, & Sketches (Ideas Library)
Drama, Skits, & Sketches 2 (Ideas Library)
Dramatic Pauses
Everyday Object Lessons
Games (Ideas Library)
Games 2 (Ideas Library)
Great Fundraising Ideas for Youth Groups
More Great Fundraising Ideas for Youth Groups
Great Retreats for Youth Groups
Greatest Skits on Earth
Greatest Skits on Earth, Vol. 2
Holiday Ideas (Ideas Library)
Hot Illustrations for Youth Talks
More Hot Illustrations for Youth Talks
Still More Hot Illustrations for Youth Talks
Incredible Questionnaires for Youth Ministry
Junior High Game Nights
More Junior High Game Nights
Kickstarters: 101 Ingenious Intros to Just about Any Bible Lesson

Live the Life! Student Evangelism Training Kit
Memory Makers
Play It! Great Games for Groups
Play It Again! More Great Games for Groups
Special Events (Ideas Library)
Spontaneous Melodramas
Super Sketches for Youth Ministry
Teaching the Bible Creatively
The Next Level: Youth Leader's Kit
Videos That Teach
What Would Jesus Do? Youth Leader's Kit
Wild Truth Bible Lessons
Wild Truth Bible Lessons 2
Wild Truth Bible Lessons—Pictures of God
Worship Services for Youth Groups

Discussion Starters
Discussion & Lesson Starters (Ideas Library)
Discussion & Lesson Starters 2 (Ideas Library)
Get 'Em Talking
Keep 'Em Talking!
High School TalkSheets
More High School TalkSheets
High School TalkSheets: Psalms and Proverbs
Junior High TalkSheets
More Junior High TalkSheets
Junior High TalkSheets: Psalms and Proverbs
What If...? 450 Thought-Provoking Questions to Get Teenagers Talking,
    Laughing, and Thinking
Would You Rather...? 465 Provocative Questions to Get Teenagers Talking
Have You Ever...? 450 Intriguing Questions Guaranteed to Get
    Teenagers Talking

Clip Art
ArtSource: Stark Raving Clip Art (print)
ArtSource: Youth Group Activities (print)
ArtSource CD-ROM: Clip Art Library Version 2.0

Videos
EdgeTV
The Heart of Youth Ministry: A Morning with Mike Yaconelli
Purpose-Driven Youth Ministry Video Curriculum
Next Time I Fall in Love Video Curriculum
Understanding Your Teenager Video Curriculum

Student Books
Grow For It Journal
Grow For It Journal through the Scriptures
Spiritual Challenge Journal: The Next Level
Teen Devotional Bible
What Would Jesus Do? Spiritual Challenge Journal
Wild Truth Journal for Junior Highers
Wild Truth Journal—Pictures of God